adds value to business,
work and life.

Employers are responsible for providing a safe and healthful workplace for their employees. OSHA's role is to assure the safety and health of America's employees by setting and enforcing standards; providing training, outreach and education; establishing partnerships; and encouraging continual improvement in workplace safety and health.

This handbook provides a general overview of a particular topic related to OSHA standards. It does not alter or determine compliance responsibilities in OSHA standards or the *Occupational Safety and Health Act of 1970*. Because interpretations and enforcement policy may change over time, you should consult current OSHA administrative interpretations and decisions by the Occupational Safety and Health Review Commission and the Courts for additional guidance on OSHA compliance requirements.

This information is available to sensory impaired individuals upon request. Voice phone: (202) 693-1999; teletypewriter (TTY) number: (877) 889-5627.

Edwin G. Foulke, Jr.
Assistant Secretary of Labor for
Occupational Safety and Health

Ethylene Oxide (EtO):
Understanding OSHA's
Exposure Monitoring Requirements

Making the Right Decisions –
How to Comply with the EtO Standard

U.S. Department of Labor

Occupational Safety and Health Administration

OSHA 3325-01N
2007

Contents

Purpose

The purpose of this guidance document is to help employers understand how to monitor the quality of the air in workplaces where ethylene oxide (EtO) is processed, used, or handled. Air monitoring is an important activity that can help alert employers when unsafe levels of EtO are present in the air so that they can take steps to reduce employee exposure. EtO can be used more safely if appropriate precautions are taken and if equipment is adequately designed and maintained. This document:

- Clarifies the different types of EtO exposure monitoring,
- Lists and explains the exposure levels used by OSHA,
- Reviews the exposure monitoring requirements in OSHA's EtO rules, and
- Outlines the monitoring decisions that the employer needs to make when employees work in areas where EtO is present.

All of the required actions presented in this document are based on OSHA's EtO standard (29 CFR 1910.1047). This guidance document provides helpful suggestions for complying with §1910.1047 as well.

This guidance document is not a standard or regulation, and it creates no new legal obligations. The guidance document is advisory in nature, informational in content, and is intended to assist employers in providing a safe and healthful workplace. The Occupational Safety and Health Act requires employers to comply with hazard-specific safety and health standards promulgated by OSHA or by a State with an OSHA-approved State Plan. In addition, pursuant to Section 5(a)(1), the General Duty Clause of the Act, employers must provide their employees with a workplace free from recognized hazards likely to cause death or serious physical harm. Employers can be cited for violating the General Duty Clause if there is a recognized hazard and they do not take reasonable steps to prevent or abate the hazard. However, failure to implement these recommendations is not, in itself, a violation of the General Duty Clause. Citations can only be based on standards, regulations, and the General Duty Clause.

Background

EtO is used extensively by hospitals and other industries as a sterilizing agent. EtO is a colorless, odorless gas which is both flammable and highly reactive. Most importantly, you cannot smell EtO until it reaches levels that can cause serious harm to human health (NIOSH, 1989). Human and animal studies consistently show that EtO can be hazardous to human health. Short-term exposures to EtO can cause respiratory irritation and lung injury, shortness of breath, headache, nausea, vomiting, and diarrhea. Long-term exposure over many years may cause cancer, reproductive effects, genetic changes, and damage to the nervous system (Lamontagne et al., 1990).

OSHA Requirement for Air Monitoring

The OSHA EtO standard requires employers to conduct personal monitoring unless they are specifically exempt (see "Exemptions" text box at page 10). This guidance document is intended to help employers understand the difference between personal monitoring, area monitoring, and leak detection and why area monitoring is complementary to personal monitoring, but can never be used instead of it.

Clarifying the Different Types of Exposure Monitoring

There are three types of EtO monitoring available for determining levels of EtO in a workplace: 1) personal monitoring, 2) area monitoring, and 3) leak detection (a special type of area monitoring). However, personal monitoring is required to determine if there is compliance with the exposure limits of the standard.

Personal Monitoring

Personal monitoring involves measuring a person's exposure to EtO by testing the air that the person (an employee) would breathe regardless of where the person moves in the workplace. A sampling device is attached to the shirt collar or as close as practical to the nose and mouth of the employee in the employee's "breathing zone" – the hemisphere forward of the shoulders with a radius of approximately six to nine inches – to test airborne EtO concentrations.

The device is worn for a specified period of time. During personal monitoring for EtO, the sample is collected for 15 minutes to test short-term exposure or for the length of a whole work shift (typically 8 hours; see the text box "What if the Work Shift is Not Exactly 8 Hours?" at page 8) to test for average exposures over the course of a workday. These air samples will be referred to here as 15-minute samples and 8-hour samples.

Equipment used for personal monitoring typically includes a "passive diffusion monitor" (a type of clip-on tag that collects EtO), or alternatively a small air pump worn on the employee's belt that pulls a sample of air through a glass tube filled with a substance that captures EtO. These samples typically must be sent to a laboratory for analysis. The accuracy of any method depends to a large degree upon the skills and experience of those who not only collect the samples but also those who analyze the samples.

After the samples have been analyzed, the employer must post monitoring results within 15 days of receiving them, or notify employees of the results in writing. The employer must also mention the steps being taken to reduce employee exposures when the monitoring results indicate that the time-weighted average or excursion limit has been exceeded.

Area Monitoring

Area monitoring is used to show the levels of EtO throughout the general working area and to identify problems and priorities.

Area samples should be taken close to a source of emission in order to evaluate concentrations or the effectiveness of steps taken to control exposure. Alternatively, area samples can be collected at

5

www.osha.gov

various places in the working area to assess how far EtO might have spread. Equipment used for area monitoring is often mounted on the wall or placed directly on equipment. The monitoring instrumentation can be similar to that used for personal monitoring, or it can be of the "direct-reading" type, which gives an immediate reading of the EtO level. When an employer uses direct reading instruments, nothing needs to be sent to a laboratory but the equipment must be calibrated periodically to ensure accuracy.

A wall-mounted emergency alert system used for area monitoring is one example of a direct-reading area monitor (also see subsection titled "Emergency Alert Provision" at page 18).

Leak Detection

Employers, who are required to create a written compliance program because their employees' exposures are over the permissible exposure limit, must also produce a schedule for routine leak detection surveys. Some businesses that use EtO find it helpful to test equipment such as sterilizers, pipes, tanks, and fittings at least every two weeks to confirm that there are no leaks. Portable EtO gas-detection meters are available to check for leaks around equipment such as sterilizers, tanks, fittings, and pipes that contain EtO. Leak testing is generally performed using hand-held EtO detection meters (a type of portable direct-reading instrument).

The OSHA Exposure Levels

The Federal OSHA regulation on EtO establishes certain allowable exposure levels. This section will explain the terms, units, and exposure levels that require action.

Units of Measure: Exposure levels are reported as concentrations – the volume of EtO per volume of air. This is typically expressed as "parts per million" (also called "ppm"). One part per million means that there is one part of EtO in every million parts of air sampled. Alternatively, the concentration of EtO can also be reported using metric units, in milligrams of EtO per cubic meter

of air (mg/m³). It is important to compare only exposure values that have the same units of measure. For example, only compare exposure results reported as ppm to the OSHA levels for EtO reported in ppm.

Action Level: The "action level" is the 8-hour exposure level that triggers certain actions under OSHA's EtO standard. If an employee's 8-hour sample result is equal to or greater than the action level, the employer must start certain required activities such as exposure monitoring and medical surveillance.

The action level for EtO is 0.5 ppm (which equals 0.9 mg/m³).

Actions an employer must take if the personal monitoring test result is greater than, or equal to, the "action level" are outlined in the subsection titled "Actions Triggered by Air Sample Results" at page 15.

Permissible Exposure Limit (PEL): This is the exposure level of EtO above which no employees may be exposed to under normal workplace conditions. You should become familiar with two PELs; one for 8-hour samples and one for 15-minute samples.

Eight-Hour Time-Weighted Average (8-hour TWA) — This is an 8-hour (or full work shift) sample that represents the maximum average EtO levels that an employee should be exposed to.

The 8-hour PEL for EtO is 1 ppm (which equals 1.8 mg/m³).

Excursion Limit (15-minute) — This is a 15-minute (short-term) sample that represents the maximum EtO exposure level that an employee may be exposed to for a short period of time.

Rotating employees to different workstations so that they are not exposed to higher EtO levels is not an accepted way of meeting the 8-hour TWA or the Excursion Limit requirement.

The 15-minute Excursion Limit for EtO is 5 ppm (equal to 9 mg/m³).

Both types of samples are important because, taken together, they help employers protect employees over the range of exposure

conditions that employees are likely to experience. Actions that an employer must take if these PELs are exceeded are outlined in Tables 3 and 4 at pages 15-17.

What if the Work Shift is Not Exactly 8 Hours?

When you collect an 8-hour sample, OSHA expects you to collect the sample for the length of the whole work shift, no matter how long it is. The shift might be more or less than 8 hours. Although not every sample will be exactly 8 hours, the OSHA action level and 8-hour permissible exposure limit must only be compared to an 8-hour sample result.

To avoid confusion caused by samples collected for more or less time, OSHA allows you to use a simple equation that converts any full-shift sample result to an 8-*hour equivalent result* (also called an 8-hour time-weighted average or an 8-hour TWA result).

Equation:

$$C_8 = C_A(T_A)/T_8$$

T_A = The actual time during which your sample was collected (in minutes).

C_A = The actual result (concentration) for your sample (in ppm).

T_8 = 480 minutes (this is the number of minutes in 8 hours).

C_8 = The 8-hour equivalent result for your sample (in ppm).

Fortunately, most analytical laboratories will do the calculation for you. Ask the laboratory to "Report the full-shift results as 8-hour time-weighted averages (or 8-hour TWAs)." You do not need to make this arrangement for 15-minute samples, which should always be collected for exactly 15 minutes.

When exposure levels are high, it may be necessary to collect a series of mid-length samples (for example, 1-2 hours each) instead of a single 8-hour sample for an employee. In this case, ask the laboratory to combine all the results from one employee to create a single 8-hour TWA result.

Monitoring Requirements

- **What types of monitoring are required to be in compliance with OSHA's EtO standard?**

The OSHA EtO standard requires that each employer whose workplace does not meet the "exemption" clause, §1910.1047(a)(2), must perform personal monitoring to show whether EtO exposures are exceeding the 8-hour and/or the 15-minute PEL. The OSHA standard requires that these samples be "representative" of EtO exposures (see "Criteria for Using Results from Similar Work Conditions" text box, at page 11). There are two types of monitoring requirements: *initial* and *periodic*.

Initial Monitoring

- **Do I need to collect initial EtO samples?**

Yes. If you are not exempt (see "Exemptions" text box at page 10) and there is reason to believe that exposure levels may equal or be above the action level under "expected conditions of operation," then you are required to conduct personal EtO monitoring to accurately measure the airborne concentrations of EtO. Most employers should assume that exposure levels may reach or exceed the action level and that they must conduct exposure monitoring: 1) if their business involves processing, using, or handling products containing EtO; 2) if they are not exempt as described in the Exemption text box; and 3) if they have never conducted personal monitoring.

This level of caution is important because accidental releases of EtO may occur from several sources, including leaking cartridges, sterilizer discharge lines and leaks, or routine changing of EtO supply cylinders. A relatively small quantity of EtO released into an average office-sized space can result in concentrations that are many times above the action level or PEL (NIOSH, 1989; Lamontagne and Kelsey 1998). If there are special circumstances that would suggest that monitoring is not required for your workplace and you need further clarification, we encourage you to

contact your local area OSHA office. Locate your local area OSHA office by phone at 1-800-321-OSHA or online at http://www.osha.gov/html/ RAmap.html.

When carrying out initial monitoring, you must collect both **8-hour samples** (full work shift) and **15-minute samples** (short-term). At least one sample of each type is required for:

- Each work shift,
- Each job classification, and
- In each work area of the workplace.

Exemptions

Is Monitoring Always Required?

No. An employer is exempt from the standard and, therefore, is not required to conduct employee exposure monitoring if "objective data" demonstrates the processing, use, or handling of products containing EtO are not capable of releasing EtO in concentrations at or above the OSHA action level or in excess of the excursion limit under expected conditions that will cause the greatest possible release.

The objective data might include specific information generated by an individual employer or obtained from chemical manufacturers, industry studies, or trade associations that documents why your facility's processing, use, or handling of EtO would not result in workplace concentrations exceeding the action level or excursion limit.

Objective data records *must* be kept as long as the employer relies on the data to demonstrate that monitoring is not required. The types of information that should be kept include:

- The source of the objective data,
- The testing protocol, results, and/or analysis of data,
- The exempted operation and corresponding information supporting the exemption, and
- Any other data relevant to the operations, materials, processes, or employee exposures covered by the exemption.

- **Do I need to collect initial personal monitoring samples for every single employee, on every work shift?**

No. But you do need to determine the exposure level of every employee. If you have only one employee, or just a few who all do different jobs, you need to collect personal samples for each employee. However, if you have two or more employees who do the same job, you may be able to collect personal samples for one of these employees and use the results to document exposure levels for all of these employees. This is known as representative sampling. To decide whether the results for one employee will represent the EtO exposure of other employees in the group, you must evaluate certain criteria (see "Criteria for Using Results from Similar Work Conditions" text box).

If the answer is "no" to any of the questions, you probably need to compare a smaller and more similar group of employees, or conduct individual personal monitoring for each employee. If the answer to all of these questions is "yes," you may use the results from one or more employee to represent the exposure of other employees in the group. However, you must select the employee who is likely to have the highest EtO exposure (due to slight variations in work area, work practices, or experience).

Criteria for Using Results from Similar Work Conditions

- Do the employees do the same work?
- Are their working conditions similar (for example, do the employees use similar equipment and EtO products?)
- Do the employees have similar work practices, with similar EtO control measures?
- Do they work in the same area or in areas with similar air movement patterns?
- Do the employees use the same EtO product for the same amount of time during their shifts?
- Do the employees work the same distance from possible sources of EtO?

You must also keep a record stating your reasons for selecting an employee from one work shift to represent employees on another shift. One way to document the similarity of shifts is by sampling employees on each shift one time to show that the employee exposures are the same on each shift. If the exposures are the same, you can conduct future required periodic sampling on a single shift and consider it representative of all shifts. You may use this option with 8-hour samples and with 15-minute samples.

- **Am I permitted to use results of air samples collected at another time or at a different location from my initial monitoring results?**

Yes, but the work conditions must have been similar on the two dates, or at the two locations. The text box "Criteria for Using Results from Similar Work Conditions" also applies in this situation. Again, if the answer is "no" to one or more of the questions, it is likely that you must conduct initial monitoring. If the answer is "yes," then OSHA allows you to meet the initial monitoring requirements by using personal monitoring results collected for other employees at an earlier date or at a different location in the workplace. Be sure to keep a document explaining why it was appropriate to use those results.

- **Which 15-minute period should I monitor?**

You must collect a 15-minute air sample during the portion of the work shift when you think that the employee's EtO exposure will be the highest. You may need to collect several 15-minute samples during the same shift (see text box "Why Is It So Important to Collect 15-Minute Samples?").

Why Is It So Important to Collect 15-Minute Samples?

Research suggests that EtO exposures above the 15-minute OSHA PEL continue to occur in workplaces that are involved in processing, using, or handling products containing EtO. Recent studies have also shown that personal monitoring activities often fail to detect accidental exposures during EtO

leaks and spills (Lamontagne et al., 2004; Lamontagne and Kelsey 1998). Therefore, it is important to carefully consider the types of activities for which 15-minute monitoring are most useful. The following examples should provide some guidance:

- A common situation in which accidental exposures to EtO might occur involves changing EtO supply cylinders. Consider collecting 15-minute personal samples while the employees being sampled are replacing EtO cylinders.

- Employees who work directly with, or in close proximity to, EtO sterilizers or similar equipment should be monitored frequently for short-term (i.e., 15-minute) exposures to EtO at the times when they are most likely to experience exposure (such as when the employee opens the door at the end of the cycle, or while EtO is being pumped in or out of the equipment).

Periodic Monitoring

- **Do I need to repeat the EtO personal monitoring and, if so, what is the monitoring schedule?**

The answer depends on the results of initial personal monitoring for EtO. Under certain situations, a long-term schedule for personal monitoring for EtO must be established. Tables 1 and 2 provide the "periodic monitoring" schedule required by the EtO standard. The personal monitoring results might also trigger other requirements that are listed in Tables 3 and 4, which appear later in this guidance document.

Table 1 – Schedule for OSHA Exposure Monitoring	
If your initial employee monitoring results...	Then...
...show that employee exposure is below the 8-hour action level,	Discontinue monitoring for only those employees whose exposures are represented by the initial monitoring.

If your initial employee monitoring results...	Then...
...are between the 8-hour action level (0.5 ppm) and the 8-hour permissible exposure limit (PEL) of 1 ppm (including the value 0.5 ppm),	Conduct additional 8-hour personal exposure monitoring at least every 6 months.
...are above the 8-hour PEL of 1 ppm or above the 15-minute PEL of 5 ppm,	Conduct additional personal exposure monitoring (either 8-hour or 15-minute, depending on the sample type that initially exceeded the limit) at least every 3 months.

Table 2 – Requirements for Discontinuing Monitoring	
If your periodic employee monitoring results had been above the PEL (either the 8-hour TWA or the 15-minute excursion limit) and...	**Then...**
...are now *between* the 8-hour action level (0.5 ppm) and the 8-hour PEL of 1 ppm (including the value 0.5 ppm) for two consecutive tests (these samples must be collected at least 7 days apart, but no more than 3 months apart),	You can decrease the 8-hour personal monitoring frequency from every 3 months to every 6 months. Note: if 15-minute exposures exceed the excursion limit of 5 ppm, you will still need to conduct the 15-minute (excursion limit) monitoring at least every 3 months.
...are now less than the 8-hour action level (0.5 ppm) for two consecutive tests (the samples must be collected at least 7 days apart, but no more than 3 months apart),	You are no longer required to conduct periodic personal monitoring unless a change in the workplace makes additional monitoring necessary.
...now indicate that employee exposures are at or below the 15-minute PEL of 5 ppm (the excursion limit) for two consecutive tests (the samples must be collected at least 7 days apart, but no more than 3 months apart),	You may discontinue 15-minute (excursion limit) monitoring for those employees whose exposures are represented by the initial monitoring.
For definitions of OSHA Exposure Levels, see page 6.	

When must I resume air monitoring?

You must start monitoring again whenever there is a change that may result in new or additional exposures to EtO. Examples of changes that should be evaluated to determine if they may result in new or additional exposures and, therefore, would trigger resuming EtO sampling include:

- Changing EtO process equipment or increasing the volume of EtO used,
- Modifying the exhaust ventilation system,
- Hiring new or inexperienced employees, and
- Changing work practices.

You also must resume sampling any time that you have a reason to suspect that such a change may result in new or additional exposures.

Actions Triggered by Air Sample Results

I received air sampling results; now what do I do?

Tables 3 and 4 provide the lists of actions you need to take as a result of EtO monitoring results that exceed specific levels. These actions are based on the OSHA action level and/or PELs (8-hour and/or 15-minute samples).

Table 3 – Actions Triggered by Air Sample Results				
Result interpretation:	8-hour sample is equal to or above Action Level	8-hour sample is above Permissible Level	15-minute sample is above Excursion Limit	Other OSHA Standards that Apply**
Result value:	0.5 ppm or greater	Above 1 ppm	Above 5 ppm	
Action Triggered by Monitoring Results				
Provide medical surveillance (if employee's exposure is more than 30 days per year)*	Yes	Yes	Not required	1910.1020
Provide information and training	Yes	Yes	Yes	–

Establish a regulated area	Not required	Yes	Yes, also if *expected* to exceed this level	–
Take steps to reduce exposure levels with engineering controls or other methods	Not required	Yes	Yes	–
Develop and put into action a written compliance program for reducing exposure and establishing a schedule for periodic leak detection	Not required	Yes	Yes	--
Provide respirators	Not required	Yes	Yes	1910.134
Ensure that caution labels are fixed to containers (also when container contents are capable of causing or can be reasonably foreseen to cause these exposure levels)	Yes	Yes	Yes	1910.1200
Establish periodic air monitoring programs	Yes, at least every 6 months	Yes, at least every 3 months	Yes, at least every 3 months	1910.1020

* Medical examinations are also required if there is an exposure related to an emergency situation.
** For information on OSHA standards that apply, see the text box titled "Important References to OSHA Standards".

Table 4 – Actions Triggered by the Air Sampling Process

Other Actions Triggered by Air Monitoring	When to Take Action	Other OSHA Standards that Apply*
Post monitoring results within 15 days of receiving them, or give employees the written results. Mention steps being taken to reduce exposures.	Any time that samples are collected – regardless of the results	1910.1020
Maintain records of monitoring for 30 years	Any time that samples are collected – regardless of the results	1910.1020

Allow employees or their representatives to observe air monitoring	Any time that samples are collected	–
* For information on OSHA standards that apply, see the text box titled "Important References to OSHA Standards" at page 22.		

Methods of Detecting Emergency EtO Releases

There are a number of options available on how to monitor and test for emergency leaks of EtO. These methods may be appropriate in addition to, but not instead of, personal air monitoring. They cannot be used as a substitute for personal monitoring to satisfy OSHA personal air monitoring requirements.

Emergency Situations

The OSHA EtO standard requires that a written plan for each workplace be developed for emergency situations. (See also §1910.38 Emergency Action Plans and §1910.39 Fire Prevention Plans.)

Emergency Plan for EtO

The following are some simple steps to ensure that your workplace meets the emergency plan requirements in OSHA's EtO standard:

- For employers with more than 10 employees, the emergency plan must be in writing and available to employees. If you have 10 or fewer employees, the plan may be communicated verbally to employees.

- The plan must include procedures for emergency evacuation, including type of evacuation and exit route assignments (refer to OSHA's standard for "Emergency Action Plans", listed in the text box on Important References to OSHA Standards at page 22). Although not specifically required, you can be proactive in

emergency planning preparations by conducting employee evacuation drills for potential EtO emergencies.

- You must have a system for alerting employees to emergency EtO exposures. You do have the flexibility to choose any effective method of alerting employees to potential EtO releases that could result in harmful exposures.

- The plan must specifically provide that employees engaged in correcting emergency conditions shall be equipped with respiratory protection as required by §1910.1047(g) until the emergency is abated and must be implemented in accordance with §1910.134, Respiratory Protection.

Emergency Alert Provision

The emergency alert provision of OSHA's EtO standard allows employers to choose the most effective method of alerting employees across industries. As part of the emergency plan, you must develop a system for alerting your employees. The precise type of alert system is not specified in the OSHA EtO standard.

OSHA considers the following alert methods acceptable for an EtO monitoring system:

- *A bell or other alarm system:* A bell or alarm system must have a distinctive signal to alert employees to an EtO leak (refer to §1910.165, Employee Alarm Systems).

- *A voice-activated system:* Like other alarm types, this system must have a distinctive signal to alert employees to an EtO leak.

- *Voice communications:* For those employers with 10 or fewer employees in a particular workplace, the requirements under

Monitoring Systems

Alarm systems basically function as a monitor to test the surrounding air for EtO levels.

To monitor EtO levels near sterilizers, some employers find it convenient to install a wall-mounted, or equipment-mounted system.

Commercially available alarms that monitor EtO levels and use both visual and sound alarms can alert employees in noisy or crowded areas when the level of EtO is higher than it should be.

More information about some specific types of monitoring devices can be found at page 20 under "Additional Sources of Information".

"Employee alarm systems" states that direct voice communication is an acceptable method of alerting employees, providing that all employees at their respective workstations can clearly hear the person's voice. For workplaces with more than 10 employees, simple voice communication is not acceptable.

- **Is there a specific EtO level that I should use to trigger an alert?**

OSHA has not established an "alert" level; you should choose an alert trigger level that is appropriate for your workplace. When evaluating alarms, it is important to remember that the alarm's purpose is to alert employees to unintended and hazardous EtO releases, rather than to average concentrations measured over an 8-hour work shift. It is not necessary to base the EtO alarm trigger specifically on the OSHA action level (0.5 ppm) or permissible exposure limits for 8 hours (1 ppm) or 15 minutes (5 ppm).

You should also be aware that there is a large range in the cost and sensitivity of commercially available monitors. Some systems alert employees to EtO levels greater than 20 ppm, while other highly sensitive monitoring devices can trigger an alarm at much lower levels, such as 1 ppm or even lower (NIOSH, 1989).

Researchers suggest that alarms that alert employees to accidental EtO spills or leaks can be reasonably set to levels of 20 ppm without compromising employee health and safety (Lamontagne and Kelsey, 1998).

How to Get Help with Air Monitoring

If you need help with air monitoring, contact the OSHA On-Site Consultation Services office for your area which can be searched by location, at http://www.osha.gov/dcsp/smallbusiness/consult_directory.html. This service is often free of charge to employers. Alternatively, you can hire an "industrial hygienist" consultant who specializes in workplace air monitoring. These consultants are often listed in the telephone directory under the headings for environmental monitoring or assessment. The American Industrial Hygiene

Association (AIHA) website also maintains a list of industrial hygiene consultants which can be searched by location, at www.aiha.org.

Laboratories provide analytical services and sometimes advise employers on selecting air sampling equipment and test media. Some laboratories provide the media or loan the equipment as part of the analysis package. Laboratories that analyze workplace air samples are typically listed in the telephone directory (environmental – analysis) and also on the AIHA website. When selecting a laboratory, one important question to ask is "Does your laboratory meet the accuracy requirements of OSHA's Ethylene Oxide standard?" OSHA's accuracy requirements can be found in §1910.1047(d)(6).

Additional Sources of Information

U.S. Navy web link that provides information about selecting EtO sterilizer alarm systems
http://p2library.nfesc.navy.mil/P2_Opportunity_Handbook/3_VII_2.html

Ethylene Oxide (EtO) Information
Environmental Monitoring Technology (EMT). EMT provides health and safety services to hospitals, clinics, laboratories, surgery centers, nursing homes, and general industry.
http://www.emt-online.com/LinksEto.htm

OSHA Fact Sheet on Ethylene Oxide (2002)
http://www.osha.gov/OshDoc/data_General_Facts/ethylene-oxide-factsheet.pdf

Ethylene Oxide Awareness Training
Albert Einstein College of Medicine, Department of Environmental Health and Safety
http://www.aecom.yu.edu/ehs/osha%20regulated/Ethylene%20Oxide.pdf

EZ Facts Safety On-line, Ethylene Oxide Fact Sheet (2003)
http://www.labsafety.com/refinfo/printpage.htm?page=/refinfo/
ezfacts/ezf176.htm

References

Lamontagne AD, et al 1990. Ethylene Oxide Health & Safety
Manual: Training and Reference Materials on the Safe Use of
Ethylene Oxide in Ster lizing Equipment. Second Edition. (OSHA
Docket H200C exhibit 2-9-L).

Lamontagne, AD, and Kelsey, MD. 1998. OSHA's Renewed Mandate
for Regulatory Flexibility: In Support of the 1984 Ethylene Oxide
Standard. *American Journal of Industrial Medicine*. 34: 95-104.

Lamontagne, AD, Oakes, JM, and Lopez, RN. 2004. Long-Term
Ethylene Oxide Exposure Trends in U.S. Hospitals: Relationship
with OSHA Regulatory and Enforcement Actions. *American Journal
of Public Health*. 94: (9), 1614-1619.

NIOSH. 1989. Technical Report: Control Technology for Ethylene
Oxide Sterilization in Hospitals. Report No. 89-120. National Institute
for Occupational Safety and Health. 89-120.pdf (179 pages, 4,133K).

Important References to OSHA Standards

OSHA, Ethylene Oxide Standard: 29 CFR 1910.1047
This is the standard that lists the OSHA requirements for EtO.
http://www.osha.gov/pls/oshaweb/owadisp.show_document?p_table=
STANDARDS&p_id=10070

OSHA, Emergency Action Plans: 29 CFR 1910.38
*This standard requires employers to create an emergency action plan. It
also lists details that must be considered in the emergency action plan.*
http://www.osha.gov/pls/oshaweb/owadisp.show_document?p_table=
STANDARDS&p_id=9726

OSHA, Respiratory Protection Standard: 29 CFR 1910.134
*This standard requires employers to have a written respiratory
protection program and a designated administrator for the program.
The respiratory protection program must state how respirators will be
selected, maintained, and cleaned. Employees must be medically
qualified, trained, and fit tested before they wear a respirator.*
http://www.osha.gov/pls/oshaweb/owadisp.show_document?p_table=
STANDARDS&p_id=12716

OSHA Employee Alarm Systems: 29 CFR 1910.165
*This standard lists maintenance, testing and inspection requirements
for emergency employee alarm systems.*
http://www.osha.gov/pls/oshaweb/owadisp.show_document?p_table=
STANDARDS&p_id=9819

OSHA, Access to Employee Exposure and Medical Records: 29 CFR
1910.1020
*This standard requires employers to maintain exposure and medical
records for 30 years. It also sets requirements for keeping medical
records confidential.*
http://www.osha.gov/pls/oshaweb/owadisp.show_document?p_table=
STANDARDS&p_id=10027

OSHA, Hazard Communication Standard: 29 CFR 1910.1200
*This standard requires employers to inform employees of the hazards
associated with products they might be exposed to in the workplace.
Employers must label containers and maintain material safety data
sheets (MSDSs).*
http://www.osha.gov/pls/oshaweb/owadisp.show_document?p_table=
STANDARDS&p_id=10099

www.osha.gov

OSHA Assistance

OSHA can provide extensive help through a variety of programs, including technical assistance about effective safety and health programs, state plans, workplace consultations, voluntary protection programs, strategic partnerships, training and education, and more. An overall commitment to workplace safety and health can add value to your business, to your workplace and to your life.

Safety and Health Program Management Guidelines

Effective management of employee safety and health protection is a decisive factor in reducing the extent and severity of work-related injuries and illnesses and their related costs. In fact, an effective safety and health program forms the basis of good employee protection and can save time and money (about $4 for every dollar spent), increase productivity, and reduce employee injuries, illnesses and related workers' compensation costs.

To assist employers and employees in developing effective safety and health programs, OSHA published recommended *Safety and Health Program Management Guidelines* (54 *Federal Register* (16): 3904-3916, January 26, 1989). These voluntary guidelines apply to all places of employment covered by OSHA.

The guidelines identify four general elements critical to the development of a successful safety and health management program:

- Management leadership and employee involvement.
- Work analysis.
- Hazard prevention and control.
- Safety and health training.

The guidelines recommend specific actions, under each of these general elements, to achieve an effective safety and health program. The *Federal Register* notice is available online at www.osha.gov.

State Programs

The Occupational Safety and Health Act of 1970 (OSH Act) encourages states to develop and operate their own job safety and

health plans. OSHA approves and monitors these plans. Twenty-four states, Puerto Rico and the Virgin Islands currently operate approved state plans: 22 cover both private and public (state and local government) employment; Connecticut, New Jersey, New York and the Virgin Islands cover the public sector only. States and territories with their own OSHA-approved occupational safety and health plans must adopt standards identical to, or at least as effective as, the Federal standards.

Consultation Services

Consultation assistance is available on request to employers who want help in establishing and maintaining a safe and healthful workplace. Largely funded by OSHA, the service is provided at no cost to the employer. Primarily developed for smaller employers with more hazardous operations, the consultation service is delivered by state governments employing professional safety and health consultants. Comprehensive assistance includes an appraisal of all mechanical systems, work practices and occupational safety and health hazards of the workplace and all aspects of the employer's present job safety and health program. In addition, the service offers assistance to employers in developing and implementing an effective safety and health program. No penalties are proposed or citations issued for hazards identified by the consultant. OSHA provides consultation assistance to the employer with the assurance that his or her name and firm and any information about the workplace will not be routinely reported to OSHA enforcement staff.

Under the consultation program, certain exemplary employers may request participation in OSHA's Safety and Health Achievement Recognition Program (SHARP). Eligibility for participation in SHARP includes receiving a comprehensive consultation visit, demonstrating exemplary achievements in workplace safety and health by abating all identified hazards and developing an excellent safety and health program.

Employers accepted into SHARP may receive an exemption from programmed inspections (not complaint or accident investigation inspections) for a period of one year. For more information concerning consultation assistance, see the OSHA website at www.osha.gov.

Voluntary Protection Programs (VPP)

Voluntary Protection Programs and on-site consultation services, when coupled with an effective enforcement program, expand employee protection to help meet the goals of the OSH Act. The three levels of VPP are Star, Merit, and Star Demonstration designed to recognize outstanding achievements by companies that have successfully incorporated comprehensive safety and health programs into their total management system. The VPPs motivate others to achieve excellent safety and health results in the same outstanding way as they establish a cooperative relationship between employers, employees and OSHA.

For additional information on VPP and how to apply, contact the OSHA regional offices listed at the end of this publication.

Strategic Partnership Program

OSHA's Strategic Partnership Program, the newest member of OSHA's cooperative programs, helps encourage, assist and recognize the efforts of partners to eliminate serious workplace hazards and achieve a high level of employee safety and health. Whereas OSHA's Consultation Program and VPP entail one-on-one relationships between OSHA and individual worksites, most strategic partnerships seek to have a broader impact by building cooperative relationships with groups of employers and em-ployees. These partnerships are voluntary, cooperative relation-ships between OSHA, employers, employee representatives and others (e.g., labor unions, trade and professional associations, universities and other government agencies).

For more information on this and other cooperative programs, contact your nearest OSHA office, or visit OSHA's website at www.osha.gov.

Alliance Program

The Alliance Program enables organizations committed to work-place safety and health to collaborate with OSHA to prevent injuries and illnesses in the workplace. OSHA and the Alliance participants work together to reach out to, educate and lead the nation's employers and their employees in improving and advancing workplace safety and health.

Groups that can form an Alliance with OSHA include employers, labor unions, trade or professional groups, educational institutions and government agencies. In some cases, organizations may be building on existing relationships with OSHA that were developed through other cooperative programs.

There are few formal program requirements for Alliances and the agreements do not include an enforcement component. However, OSHA and the participating organizations must define, implement and meet a set of short- and long-term goals that fall into three categories: training and education; outreach and communication; and promoting the national dialogue on workplace safety and health.

OSHA Training and Education

OSHA area offices offer a variety of information services, such as compliance assistance, technical advice, publications, audiovisual aids and speakers for special engagements. OSHA's Training Institute in Arlington Heights, IL, provides basic and advanced courses in safety and health for Federal and state compliance officers, state consultants, Federal agency personnel, and private sector employers, employees and their representatives.

The OSHA Training Institute also has established OSHA Training Institute Education Centers to address the increased demand for its courses from the private sector and from other Federal agencies. These centers are nonprofit colleges, universities and other organizations that have been selected after a competition for participation in the program.

OSHA also provides funds to nonprofit organizations, through grants, to conduct workplace training and education in subjects where OSHA believes there is a lack of workplace training. Grants are awarded annually. Grant recipients are expected to contribute 20 percent of the total grant cost.

For more information on grants, training and education, contact the OSHA Training Institute, Office of Training and Education, 2020 South Arlington Heights Road, Arlington Heights, IL 60005, (847) 297-4810 or see "Training" on OSHA's website at www.osha.gov. For further information on any OSHA program, contact your nearest OSHA area or regional office listed at the end of this publication.

Information Available Electronically

OSHA has a variety of materials and tools available on its website at www.osha.gov. These include *eTools* such as *Expert Advisors, Electronic Compliance Assistance Tools (e-cats), Technical Links;* regulations, directives and publications; videos and other information for employers and employees. OSHA's software programs and compliance assistance tools walk you through challenging safety and health issues and common problems to find the best solutions for your workplace.

A wide variety of OSHA materials, including standards, interpretations, directives, and more, can be purchased on CD-ROM from the U.S. Government Printing Office, Superintendent of Documents, phone toll-free (866) 512-1800.

OSHA Publications

OSHA has an extensive publications program. For a listing of free or sales items, visit OSHA's website at www.osha.gov or contact the OSHA Publications Office, U.S. Department of Labor, 200 Constitution Avenue, NW, N-3101, Washington, DC 20210. Telephone (202) 693-1888 or fax to (202) 693-2498.

Contacting OSHA

To report an emergency, file a complaint or seek OSHA advice, assistance or products, call (800) 321-OSHA or contact your nearest OSHA regional or area office listed at the end of this publication. The teletypewriter (TTY) number is (877) 889-5627.

Written correspondence can be mailed to the nearest OSHA Regional or Area Office listed at the end of this publication or to OSHA's national office at: U.S. Department of Labor, Occupational Safety and Health Administration, 200 Constitution Avenue, N.W., Washington, DC 20210.

By visiting OSHA's website at www.osha.gov, you can also:

- file a complaint online,
- submit general inquiries about workplace safety and health electronically, and
- find more information about OSHA and occupational safety and health.

OSHA Regional Offices

Region I
(CT,* ME, MA, NH, RI, VT*)
JFK Federal Building, Room E340
Boston, MA 02203
(617) 565-9860

Region II
(NJ,* NY,* PR,* VI*)
201 Varick Street, Room 670
New York, NY 10014
(212) 337-2378

Region III
(DE, DC, MD,* PA, VA,* WV)
The Curtis Center
170 S. Independence Mall West
Suite 740 West
Philadelphia, PA 19106-3309
(215) 861-4900

Region IV
(AL, FL, GA, KY,* MS, NC,* SC,* TN*)
61 Forsyth Street, SW
Room 6T50
Atlanta, GA 30303
(404) 562-2300

Region V
(IL, IN,* MI,* MN,* OH, WI)
230 South Dearborn Street
Room 3244
Chicago, IL 60604
(312) 353-2220

Region VI
(AR, LA, NM,* OK, TX)
525 Griffin Street, Room 602
Dallas, TX 75202
(214) 767-4731 or 4736 x224

Region VII
(IA,* KS, MO, NE)
City Center Square
1100 Main Street, Suite 800
Kansas City, MO 64105
(816) 426-5861

Region VIII
(CO, MT, ND, SD, UT,* WY*)
1999 Broadway, Suite 1690
PO Box 46550
Denver, CO 80202-5716
(720) 264-6550

Region IX
(American Samoa, AZ,* CA,* HI,* NV,*
Northern Mariana Islands)
71 Stevenson Street, Room 420
San Francisco, CA 94105
(415) 975-4310

Region X
(AK,* ID, OR,* WA*)
1111 Third Avenue, Suite 715
Seattle, WA 98101-3212
(206) 553-5930

    * These states and territories operate their own OSHA-approved job safety and health programs (Connecticut, New Jersey, New York and the Virgin Islands plans cover public employees only). States with approved programs must have standards that are identical to, or at least as effective as, the Federal standards.

    Note: To get contact information for OSHA Area Offices, OSHA-approved State Plans and OSHA Consultation Projects, please visit us online at www.osha.gov or call us at 1-800-321-OSHA.